Houghton Mifflin Science

DiscoveryWorks

Science Workbook

Ongoing Assessment

- Investigation Reviews

Grade 4

HOUGHTON MIFFLIN

Boston • Atlanta • Dallas • Denver • Geneva, Illinois • Palo Alto • Princeton

Contributing Artists

Anthony Accardo, Barbara Epstein Eagle, Kate Gorman, Meewha Lee.

Printed in the U. S. A.

ISBN 0-618-02843-9

3 4 5 6 7 8 9 10 PO 08 07 06 05 04 03 02 01

Contents

UNIT A

EARTH'S LAND

Investigation Review
How Does Moving Water Shape the Land?

Name ______________________ Date ______________

Use the words in the box to complete each sentence.

delta	erosion	sediments	river system	weathering

1. Materials such as soil and gravel that are carried by moving water, wind, or ice are called ____________.
2. Rocks are broken into smaller pieces by the process of ____________.
3. A river and the waterways that drain into it are called a ____________.
4. The triangular-shaped deposit formed when a river empties into the ocean is a ____________ .
5. Moving water, wind, and moving ice pick up and carry soil and other materials in a process known as ____________.

Choose the correct word so that the second pair of words is related in the same way as the first pair of words.

6. Rain is to hill as waves are to ____________.
   shoreline plants sea wall
7. Jetties are to beaches as headlands are to ____________.
   islands sea walls bays
8. Plants are to weathering as moving water is to ____________.
   beach erosion gravity
9. Boulder is to rock as river is to ____________.
   wind stream valley

Process Skills
Making and Using Models

What caused the valley to form in the activity Hills and Valleys? Write your answer on a separate sheet of paper.

Name ______________________ Date ______________

Circle the word or words that best complete each sentence.

1. Wind-blown sand can (erode, harden) rock surfaces.

2. (Plants, Valleys) can act as windbreaks, which slow down the wind.

3. A glacier moves rock and soil like a (wheelbarrow, bulldozer).

4. Where winds blow steadily in the same direction, (dunes, glaciers) move.

5. Moraines are deposited as glaciers (form, melt).

6. Read the steps that describe the formation of a sand dune. The steps are not in the right order. Number the steps in the correct order.

_______ The wind slows down when it strikes an object.

_______ Wind removes loose sand and silt from an area.

_______ Over time a sand dune forms.

_______ Wind deposits sediment in another area.

Process Skills

Inferring

Suppose a glacier begins to melt. What are two things you could observe when the ice is gone?

____

____

____

____

____

Investigation Review

Why Is Soil an Important Resource?

Name ______________________ Date ______________

Write the letter of the term that best matches the definition.

____	**1.** loose material that covers much of Earth's surface	**a.**	conservation
____	**2.** any of Earth's useful materials	**b.**	terracing
____	**3.** wise use of such things as oil, air, trees, and water	**c.**	gullies
____	**4.** the building of steplike ridges to prevent water runoff	**d.**	natural resource
____	**5.** miniature river valleys	**e.**	soil

Tell what each group of words has in common.

6. weathered rock, decayed plants ______________________

7. contour plowing, terracing ______________________

8. coal, crude oil ______________________

9. flower roots, tree roots ______________________

Process Skills

Communicating

If your job were to conserve Earth's soil, what would you say to farmers to convince them that contour plowing, strip cropping, and terracing help prevent soil erosion?

____

____

____

____

Investigation Review

Why Are Rocks and Minerals Important?

Name ______________________________ Date ____________________

Circle the letter of the word that best completes each sentence.

1. One of the properties of a mineral is ____.

a. dampness **b.** expense **c.** hardness **d.** cleanliness

2. Earth's crust is made mostly of ____.

a. rock **b.** water **c.** air **d.** ice

3. A mineral used in pencils is ____.

a. calcite **b.** graphite **c.** granite **d.** halite

4. Use the clues and the words below to complete the puzzle.

magnet	**salt**	**mineral**
rock	**ore**	**granite**

Down

1. Object to which certain minerals are attracted
2. A mineral called halite
3. A rock that can be mined for the minerals it contains
6. Solid substance made up of one or more minerals

Across

4. Natural solid substance, such as gold, found in Earth's crust
5. Hard rock often used in buildings

Process Skills

Making Inferences, Communicating

How would a room in your home look different if the world ran out of metals? Write your answer on a separate sheet of paper.

Investigation Review
Why Are Energy Resources So Important?

Name ______________________________ Date ____________________

Circle the word or words that best complete each sentence.

1. Energy is produced when (fuel, rock) burns.

2. An example of a fossil fuel is (wood, petroleum).

3. Fossil fuels are (renewable, nonrenewable) resources.

4. If the fuel called peat is buried long enough, it changes into (crude oil, coal).

5. The good news about fossil fuels is that their supplies are (dependable, unlimited).

6. A windmill farm uses wind to produce (heat, electricity).

7. A marshmallow cooked by the Sun is an example of the use of (solar energy, fossil fuel).

8. Read the steps that describe the process by which oil and natural gas form. Number the steps in the correct order.

____ **a.** Tiny once living things in the sea sink to the ocean bottom.

____ **b.** Over millions of years, heat and pressure change the dead matter into petroleum and natural gas.

____ **c.** Tiny ocean life dies.

____ **d.** Tiny living things exist in the ocean.

____ **e.** Mud and sand cover the dead organisms.

Process Skills
Communicating

In the space below, use the word *nonrenewable* in a sentence that shows you understand the meaning of the term.

____

____

Investigation Review
What Do People Throw Away, and Where Does It Go?

INVESTIGATION 1 CHAPTER 3

Name ______________________________ Date ________________

1. Use the words in the box to complete the sentences.

air	**incineration**	**ash**
landfill	**electricity**	**soil**

Most trash is buried in a(n) ______________, which is a large hole in the ground that has a liner. The trash is buried by layers of ______________.

People also dispose of trash by burning it. Burning, or ______________, turns trash to ______________, heat, and smoke. People can use the heat to produce ______________. However, burning can be a problem because the smoke can make the ______________ dirty.

2. Complete the diagram. Write characteristics of dumps and characteristics of landfills. In the part of the diagram that overlaps, write characteristics that both dumps and landfills have in common.

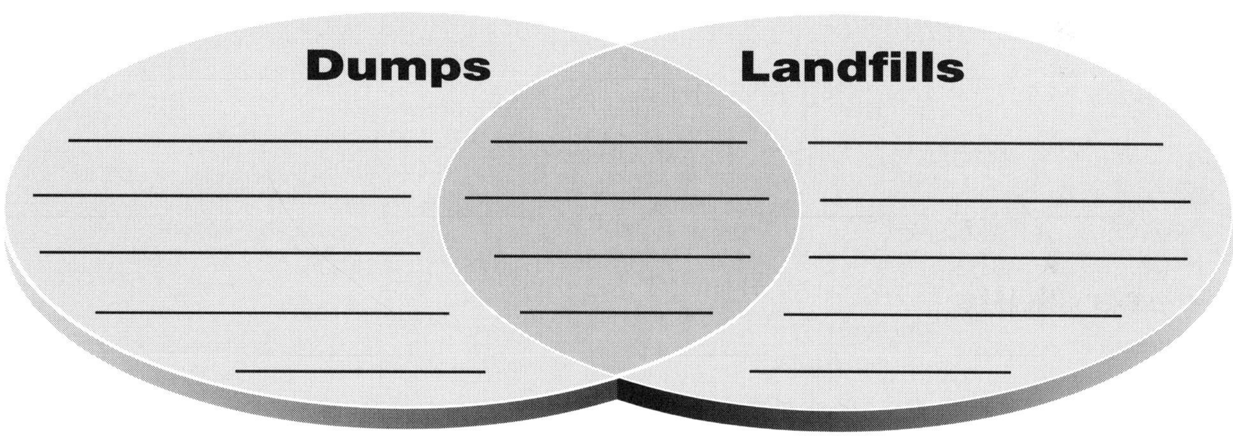

Process Skills
Making and Using a Model, Interpreting Data

How did the model you made in "Making a Landfill" help you understand the difference between landfills and dumps? Write your answer on a separate sheet of paper.

Investigation Review

How Can Trash Affect Resources?

Name ______________________________ Date ____________________

Write the letter of the phrase on the right that correctly completes each phrase on the left.

1. Using only one side of a sheet of paper is a ____.

2. Tossing a soda can into a trash can rather than putting it in a recycling bin is a ____.

3. Throwing a plastic bottle into a trash can can be thought of as a ____.

a. waste of metals

b. waste of petroleum

c. waste of trees

Choose the correct word or words so that the second pair of words is related in the same way as the first pair of words.

4. Desk is to wood as plastic bottle is to ____________________.

glass   unbreakable   petroleum

5. Germs are to human body as litter is to ____________________.

trash   environment   garbage

6. Coal is to resource as spilled oil is to ____________________.

can   grease   hazardous waste

Process Skills

Inferring

Suppose that on a beach you see more plastic litter than any other kind. Write how you might explain this.

____

____

____

____

____

Name ______________________________ Date ________________

Use the words in the box to answer each question.

aluminum	light bulbs	PET	rethinking

1. What kind of soft-drink cans can be melted down? ____________

2. What is the easiest plastic to recycle? ____________

3. What contains a kind of glass that can't be recycled? ____________

4. What process involves making choices before buying or using a product? ____________

5. The picture shows the process of recycling plastic. In the box are the lettered steps of the process. On the line under each part of the picture, write the letter of the pictured step.

a. bead-shaped pieces **c. chopping and washing** **e. drying**

b. melting and shaping **d. carried along a belt**

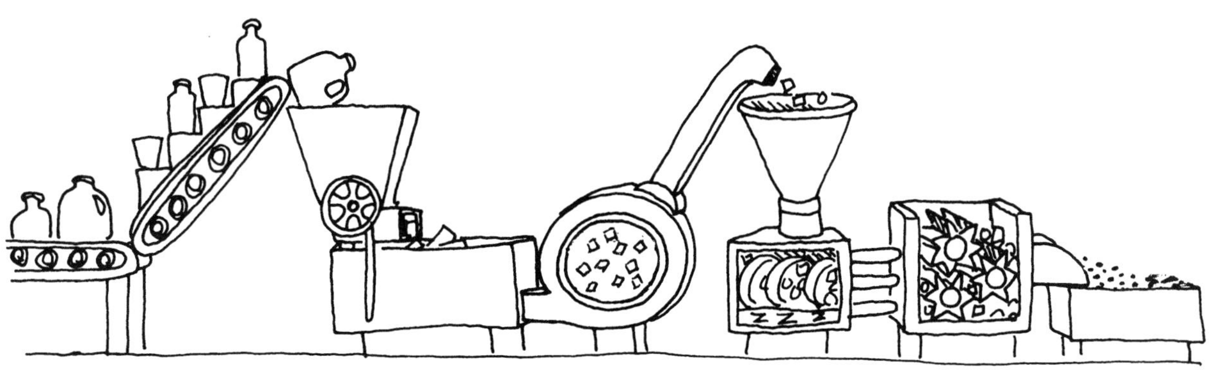

__________ __________ __________ __________ __________

Process Skills

Inferring

Why do you think it is important to recycle products made from aluminum and petroleum? Write your answer on a separate sheet of paper.

UNIT B

POPULATIONS AND ECOSYSTEMS

Name ____________________ Date ____________________

For items 1–6, identify each factor below as either biotic or abiotic.

1. ladybird beetle __________
2. snow __________
3. maple tree __________
4. earthworm __________
5. rock __________
6. mosquito __________

7. Use the terms in the box to complete the concept map below.

soil	**abiotic**	**community**	**populations**
temperature	**biotic**	**rocks**	**species**

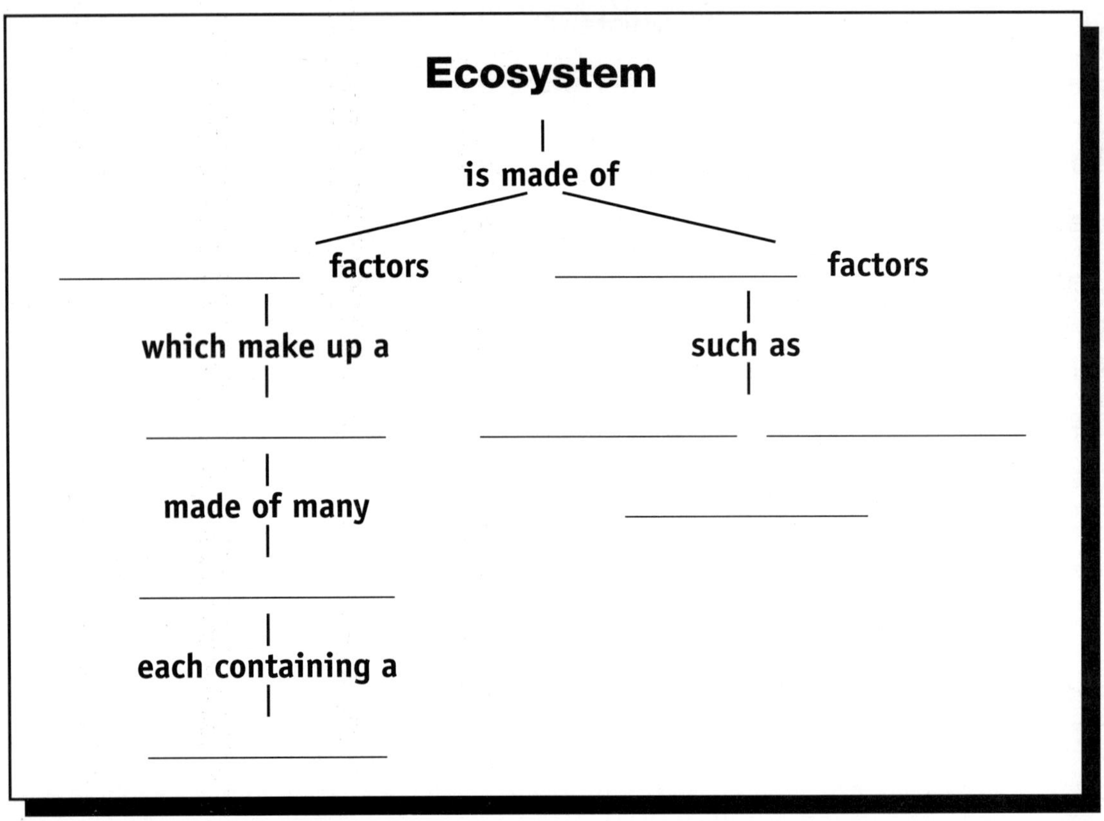

Process Skills

Observing

How could you determine that living things in a wooded area interact with each other? Write your answer on a separate sheet of paper.

Investigation Review
What Do We Throw Away and Where Does It Go?

Name ______________________________ Date ______________

1. Look at the picture of a marsh ecosystem. Use the words in the box to label the picture.

consumer
producer
decomposer

Write the letter of the term that best matches the definition.

___	**2.** plant-eating animal	**a.**	consumer
___	**3.** process of using light energy to make food	**b.**	herbivore
___	**4.** organism that obtains energy by eating other organisms	**c.**	sunlight
___	**5.** common producers	**d.**	mushroom
___	**6.** long-term relationship between species	**e.**	photosynthesis
___	**7.** role of a species in an ecosystem	**f.**	plants
___	**8.** type of forest decomposer	**g.**	symbiosis
___	**9.** energy captured by plants	**h.**	niche

Process Skills
Inferring

Suppose you visit the seashore shown below. What might you infer about the relationship between the crabs and the seagulls? Write your answer on a separate sheet of paper.

Investigation Review
How Does Energy Flow In an Ecosystem?

Name ______________________ Date ______________

1. Label the ocean food web, using the terms from the box.

first-order consumer	**second-order consumer**
decomposer	**third-order consumer**
producer	**fourth-order consumer**

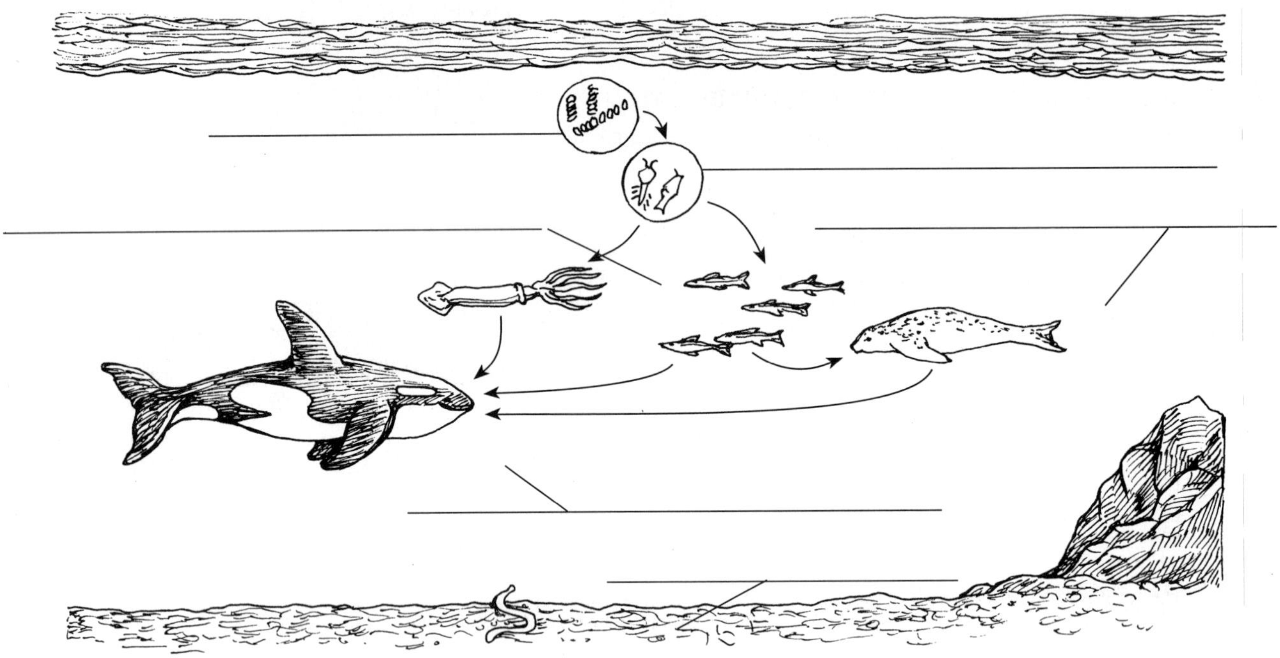

2. Under each term below, write an example of an organism from a marsh ecosystem that completes the food chain.

Producer → First-order consumer → Second-order consumer → Third-order consumer → Decomposer

________ ________ ________ ________ ________

Process Skills
Inferring, Communicating

In the Arctic, caribou search for patches of mosses and lichens. The caribou are watched by gray wolves that prey on sick or weak animals. What are the producers in this ecosystem, and how do their numbers compare to the numbers of first- and second-order consumers?

Name ______________________________ Date ____________________

For items 1–3, circle the word or words that best complete each sentence.

1. The (life cycle, water cycle) is the constant movement of water in a continuous cycle through land, sea, air, and living things.

2. The use of oxygen by a cell to break down carbon compounds and release energy is called (cell respiration, evaporation).

3. (Proteins, acids) are the compounds that act as the building blocks of living things.

For items 4–6, use the words in the box to complete each sentence.

photosynthesis	cell respiration	condensation

4. During ____________________, living things use oxygen and release carbon dioxide.

5. __________________ is the process by which water vapor changes to liquid water.

6. During ____________________, plants take in carbon dioxide and release oxygen.

Process Skills

Observing, Experimenting

Patti placed a plant inside a plastic bag. A day later she observed droplets on the inside of the bag. Then she removed a leaf and put it in a test tube with yellow BTB solution. She observed that the solution turned blue when the test tube was left in sunlight. The solution remained yellow in a second test tube containing BTB but no leaf. What two forms of matter has Patti observed being recycled by her plant? What plant processes have taken place? Why did Patti use the second test tube? Write your answers on a separate sheet of paper.

Name ______________________________ Date ____________________

1. Use the words in the box to complete the sentences.

biomes	**deciduous forests**	**desert**	**rain forests**	**tundra**

Let's take an imaginary trip around the world by thinking about the world's largest ecosystems, or ____________________. In the warmest climates, there are lush ____________________, where it rains almost every day. What a contrast to the ____________________, which can also be very hot, but where it hardly rains at all. Farther north the ____________________ grow. There the winters are cold, but the summers are warm and wet. Even farther north are the taiga, where you find coniferous forests, and the ____________________, where the subsoil stays frozen all year.

2. Write the name of a biome each of these organisms would call home.

a. __________ **b.** __________ **c.** __________ **d.** __________ **e.** __________

Process Skills

Inferring

Several students were watering some of their classroom plants on the schedule shown. Can you infer what kind of plant is in each group? Write your answer on a separate sheet of paper.

Plant Group A:
lightly, every two weeks

Plant Group B:
every 2–3 days

Name ______________________________ Date ____________________

For items 1–4, write the letter of the term that best matches the definition.

___ **1.**	gone forever as a species	**a.** biodiversity
___ **2.**	abundance of different life forms	**b.** threatened
___ **3.**	at risk of becoming endangered	**c.** endangered
___ **4.**	in danger of becoming extinct	**d.** extinct

5. Suppose you are a newspaper reporter. On a separate sheet of paper, write a headline and a few sentences about the loss of species from the rain forest. Use words such as *biodiversity*, *endangered*, *extinct*, and *threatened*.

Process Skills

Communicating, Making a Hypothesis

Hypothesize what has happened to the rain forest of the Philippines. What do you think has happened to the many species of birds and flowering plants that lived in the original rain forest? Write your answer on a separate sheet of paper.

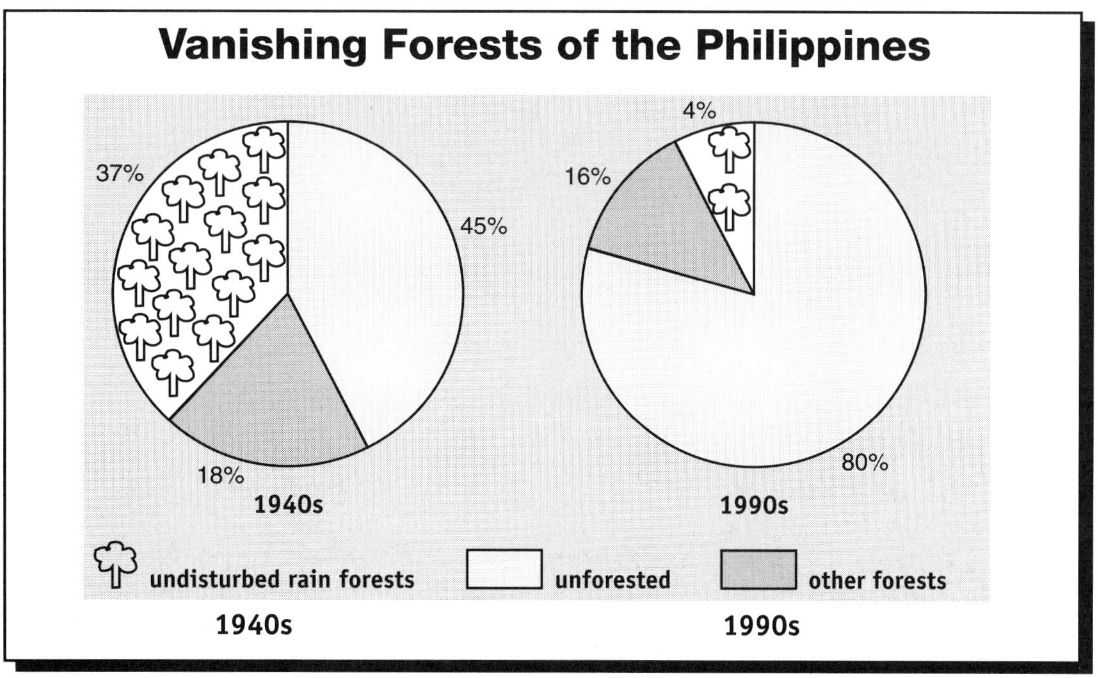

UNIT C

THE SOLID EARTH

Investigation Review
How Can You Identify Minerals?

Name ______________________________ Date ____________________

For items 1–5, write the letter of the term that best matches the definition.

____	**1.** a measure of how easily a mineral can be scratched	**a.** streak
____	**2.** the way minerals reflect light	**b.** hardness
____	**3.** a property that describes how some minerals break	**c.** color
____	**4.** the color of a powdered mineral	**d.** luster
____	**5.** the least reliable mineral property	**e.** cleavage

6. Mark wants to place six minerals in an egg carton so that the minerals with metallic luster are in the top row and those with nonmetallic luster are in the bottom row. Also, he wants to place them in order of increasing hardness. Hardness numbers are shown in parentheses. Using the information given, label his carton with the correct letters. The Mineral Properties chart may also be helpful.

a. gypsum (2)

b. quartz (7)

c. pyrite (6)

d. galena ($2\frac{1}{2}$)

e. gold (3)

f. talc (1)

Process Skills
Classifying

Gerry observed some properties of an unknown mineral specimen. He wrote his data in the chart shown. How did he test for hardness?

Color	Luster	Hardness
clear	nonmetallic (glassy)	H > glass H < topaz (7 on Mohs' scale)

____

____

Investigation Review
What Are Minerals Used For?

Name ______________________________ Date ________________

1. Use the words in the box to complete the concept map.

steel	**computer chips**	**concrete**	**glass**
minerals	**magnetite**	**hematite**	**recycled**
iron	**quartz**		

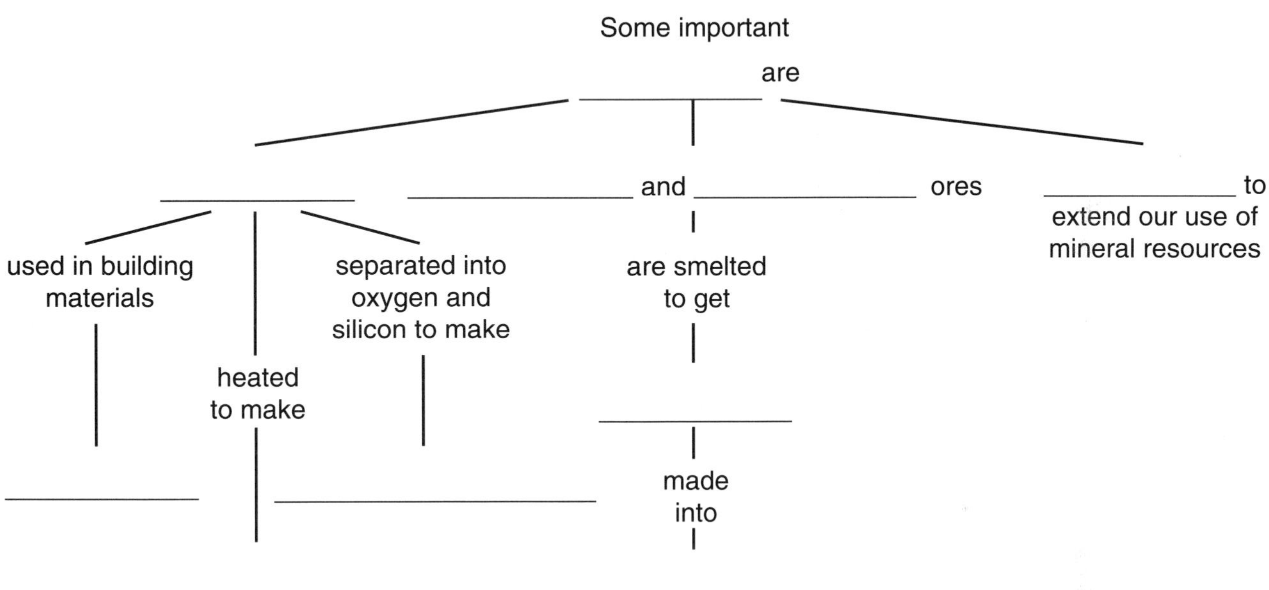

Use the clues to unscramble each word.

2. How are ores removed from the ground? g i n n i m ________________

3. Amethyst and tiger eye are gems made of this versatile mineral.

z a r t q u ________________

4. This is something that grows, but it's not alive. l a s t c r y ________________

5. How are ores treated to remove metal? l e t m s g i n ________________

Process Skills
Communicating, Inferring

Which property of mineral quartz makes it useful for making concrete? Which property allows it to be made into glass? Write your answer on a separate sheet of paper.

Name ______________________________ Date ____________________

Write the letter of the term that best matches the definition.

____ **1.** form from small bits of rocks and minerals that become cemented by natural processes

____ **2.** form when existing rocks are changed by heat, pressure, or chemicals

____ **3.** form when hot, melted material cools and hardens

a. igneous rocks

b. sedimentary rocks

c. metamorphic rocks

Write the answer to each riddle on the line provided.

4. Deep within Earth I'm called magma, but once I reach the surface I'm known as ____________.

5. I depend on how long it takes for the minerals within a rock to form. I am the rock's ____________.

6. I have been trapped in this piece of limestone for ages—even before it was a rock! I help scientists learn about organisms from the past. I am a ____________.

Process Skills

Classifying, Inferring

Suppose you have two igneous rocks containing mostly light-colored minerals. One has large mineral grains. The other has small grains. Classify and identify the two rocks using the data provided. Which rock took a longer time to form? How do you know? Which formed closer to Earth's surface? Write your answer on the lines provided.

	COMPOSITION	
	Contains more light-colored minerals	Contains more dark-colored minerals
LARGE mineral grains: forms from **MAGMA**	**Granite**	**Gabbro**
SMALL mineral grains: forms from **LAVA**	**Rhyolite**	**Basalt**

____

____

____

____

Investigation Review

How Do the Properties of Rocks Make Them Useful?

INVESTIGATION 2 CHAPTER 2

Name ______________________________ Date ____________________

For items 1 and 2, use the words in the box to complete the sentences.

clay	**dimension stone**	**marble**	**quarries**
crushed stone	**firing**	**molds**	**water**

1. Each year, billions of tons of rock are removed from ______________ all over the world. Most of the rock leaves a quarry as __________________. Some rock, known as ____________________, remains in larger pieces. Granite used in a building and a ______________ countertop are examples of dimension stone.

2. Many buildings are made of brick. Unlike rocks, bricks are made by people. The "recipe" is pretty simple. ______________ minerals and ______________ are mixed into a thick paste. The mixture is put into rectangular ______________ and placed in an oven. ______________ the bricks makes them harder.

3. Fill in the blanks of the concept map.

Two important sources for building materials are

stone from ______________

blasted to get ______________ for construction

drilled to get ______________ cut to specific sizes and shapes

______________ and sediments

which are crushed into a powder

combined with ______________

fired to make ______________

Process Skills

Hypothesizing

Suppose you observed the houses in a very old village. How could they help you hypothesize about the types of rocks that are commonly found in that region? Write your answer on a separate sheet of paper.

Investigation Review

How Do Rocks Change Over Time?

Name ______________________________ Date ____________________

Use the words in the box to complete each sentence.

anthracite	bituminous	lignite	peat

1. Temperature and pressure increase and squeeze most of the water from lignite to form ____________ coal.

2. Swamp plants decay and form a dark, watery material called ____________.

3. Metamorphism changes bituminous coal into ____________, the coal with the highest percentage of carbon.

4. Sediments squeeze much of the water out of peat, forming ____________.

Complete the diagram of the rock cycle.

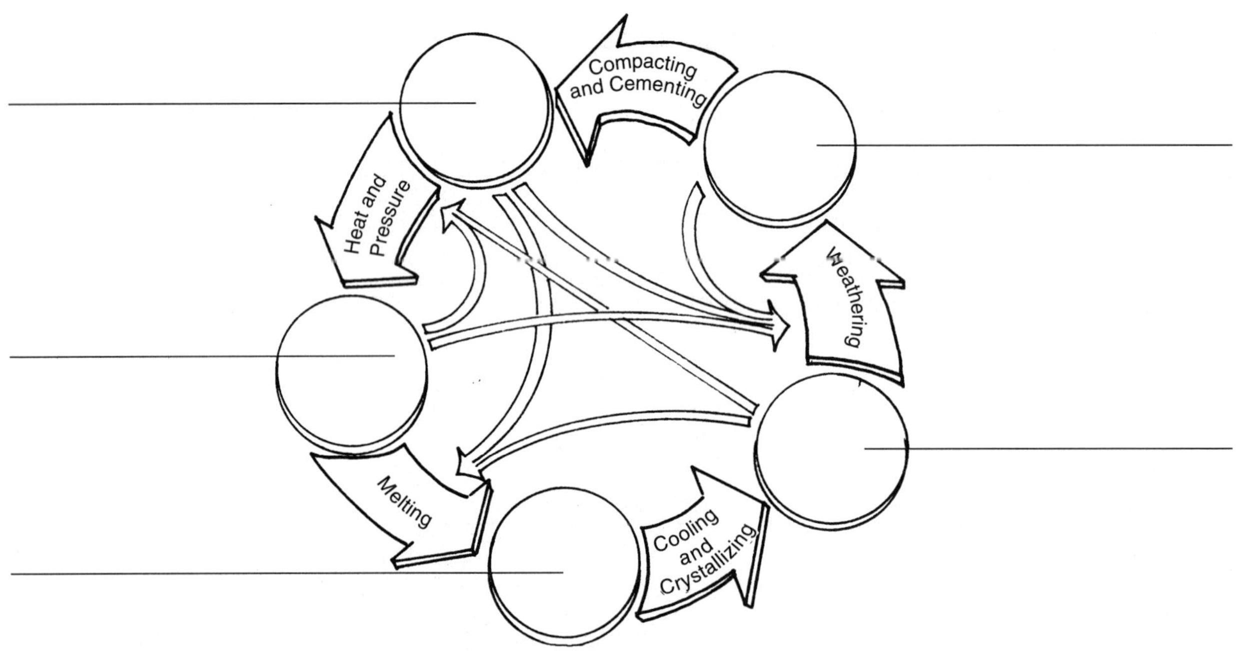

Process Skills

Communicating

List the steps involved to change an igneous rock into a sedimentary rock. Write or draw your answer on a separate sheet of paper.

Investigation Review
What Is Earth's Structure?

INVESTIGATION 1 CHAPTER 3

Name ______________________________ Date ____________________

1. If you took an imaginary journey to the center of the Earth, your trip log might read something like this. Use the words in the box to complete the sentences.

crust	iron	mantle	plates
inner	magma	outer	solid

Day 1: Today we cut through the rocky ____________, which, with the upper mantle, is broken into____________.

Day 2: We reached the ____________. It is made of igneous rock which sometimes rises toward the crust as ____________.

Day 3: We moved into the ____________ core of Earth. It is so hot here that ____________ and nickel are liquids.

Day 4: Finally! We've reached the __________ core. It is almost as hot as the Sun. The pressure here compressed melted metals into a _________ core.

2. What kinds of waves are a result of earthquakes? How are they alike? How are they different?

____

____

____

Process Skills
Making a Model

Suppose you had brown, yellow, orange, and red clay. Which colors would you use to make a model of the layers of Earth? What characteristics would you represent with each color? For which color clay would you need the greatest quantity? Write your answer on a separate sheet of paper.

Investigation Review

How Can Fossils Help Tell Us How Old a Rock Is?

Name ______________________ Date ______________

On the line under each set of terms, write what the terms have in common.

1. imprint, cast, mold

____

2. using index fossils, using potassium-argon decay

____

3. Read the stages that describe how a plant might become a fossil. Number the stages in the order in which they would occur.

____ The rock containing the fossil is eroded and exposed.

____ The plant is buried by sediments. Over time, the leaves decay, but leave an imprint in the soft sediment.

____ The plant dies.

____ Eventually the woody parts are replaced with minerals that harden to become rock.

Process Skills

Inferring

Imagine that you find two different rocks on your way home from school. They both contain the same kind of trilobite. What can you infer about the age of these two rocks? Is your inference a relative age or an absolute age? Explain.

____

____

____

____

____

Investigation Review
How Do Rocks Bend?

INVESTIGATION 3 CHAPTER 3

Name ______________________ Date ______________

For items 1–5, write the letter of the term that best matches the definition.

____ **1.** the removal of weathered rock

____ **2.** a downward fold in rocks

____ **3.** a mountain formed when rock layers are pushed up by magma

____ **4.** an upward fold in rocks

____ **5.** a bend in a rock layer

a. fold

b. anticline

c. syncline

d. erosion

e. dome

6. Use the clues and the words in the box to complete the crossword puzzle.

weathering	**plates**	**wind**	**ridges**
anticline	**hogbacks**	**folds**	**dome**

Down

1. Process that breaks rocks down into sediments

3. Rocks resistant to erosion form these

6. Bends in rock

Across

2. Formed when rock layers are pushed up by magma

4. Upward rock fold

5. Pieces of Earth's crust and upper mantle

7. A force that causes erosion

8. Another name for steep ridges

Process Skills
Inferring, Communicating

Imagine you are riding in a car. You pass some exposed rock layers made visible by blasting. The layers are in the shape of a wave. Why?

Investigation Review
What Is a Fault, and How Can It Make Mountains?

Name ______________________ Date ______________________

1. Use the words in the box to complete the sentences.

faults	**horizontal**	**earthquakes**
fault-block	**vertical**	**strike-slip**

On a trip to California, you can learn a lot about ____________, which are breaks in rocks along which movement occurs. When the movement along some faults is ____________, ____________ mountains can form. The Sierra Nevada are spectacular examples of this kind of mountain. Near the coast of California is the famous San Andreas fault. The movement along this fault is ____________, and it is known as a ____________ fault. Each year the city of Los Angeles moves several centimeters north toward San Francisco. There have been many ____________ along this fault.

2. When moving plates caused rocks in the Grand Canyon area to stretch, many normal faults were formed. The picture shows a normal fault. Label the fault line and draw arrows to show its movement.

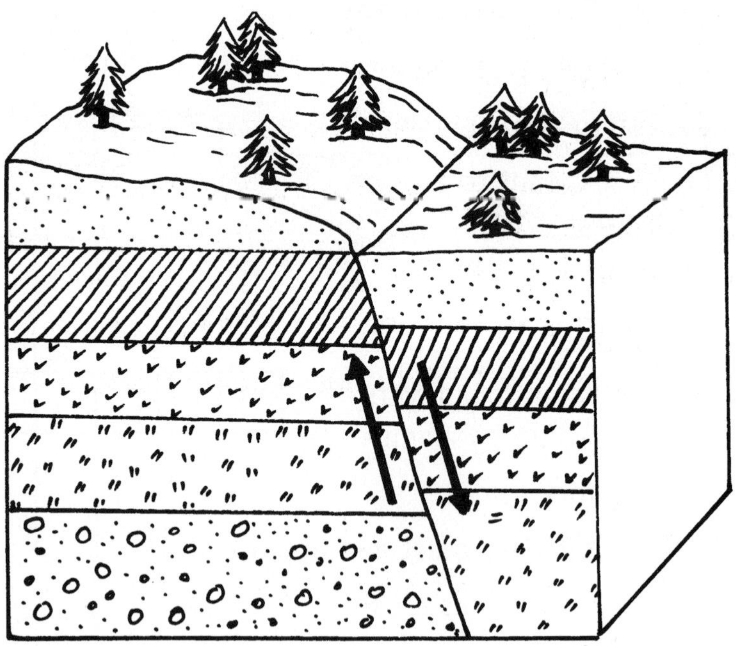

Process Skills
Making a Model

If you were holding a stack of books in each hand, how could you use them to show motion along a strike-slip fault? Write or draw your answer on a separate sheet of paper.

UNIT

D

MAGNETISM AND ELECTRICITY

Investigation Review

What Are Magnets?

Name ______________________________ Date ____________________

Use the words in the box to answer each question.

repel	attract	iron
magnetism	temporary	permanent

1. Which material is best attracted by a magnet? ____________

2. How do the north and south poles of two magnets react to each other?

____

3. What kind of magnet is made in a factory? ____________

4. What is a magnet's property of attracting certain materials called?

____

5. What kind of magnet is a magnetized iron nail? ____________

6. How do like poles of two magnets react to each other? ____________

Use the clues below to unscramble the letters of each word.

7. rising into the air

T A L E T I V I N O ________________

8. a type of magnet that doesn't keep its magnetism very long

M A P R E T R Y O ________________

9. an object that attracts materials such as iron and steel

T A M G E N ________________

10. a type of magnet that keeps its magnetism for a long time

R A N M E T P E N ________________

Process Skills

Communicating

Using the information in this Investigation, draw an invention on a separate sheet of paper that would pick up a steel fork.

Name ______________________ Date ______________

Label the drawing of the magnet shown below. Use the words in the box.

lines of force	magnetic field	north pole	south pole

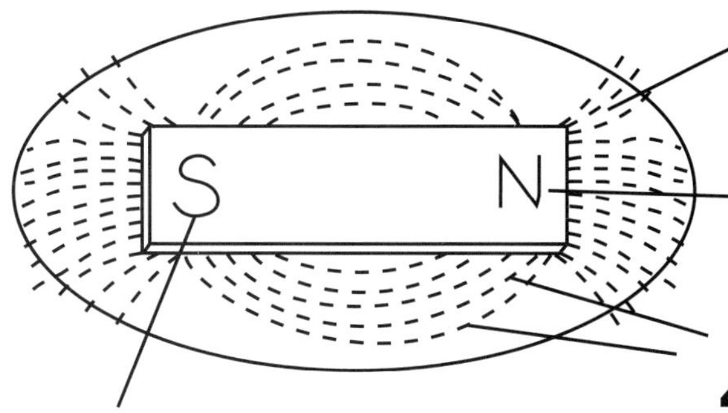

1. ______________

2. ______________

3. ______________

4. ______________

Choose the correct word so that the second pair of words are related in the same way as the first pair of words.

5. Map is to street as compass is to ______________.

needle   lost   direction

6. Lodestone is to iron nails as magnet is to ______________.

steel paper clips   paper   rubber bands

7. Magnetic north pole is to northern lights as magnetic south pole is to

______________.

magnet   southern lights   geographic south pole

8. Magnet is to visible as magnetic field is to ______________.

flat   iron   invisible

Process Skills

Predicting

What do you think would happen if you spilled some iron nails near a bar magnet? Write your answer on a separate sheet of paper.

Name ______________________ Date ______________

Circle the word or words that best complete each sentence.

1. Unlike charges (repel, attract) each other.

2. Like charges (repel, attract) each other.

3. A negatively charged balloon can stick to a wall after the (positive, negative) charges of the wall are pushed away.

4. When negative charges jump from a cloud to the ground, (lightning, rain) occurs.

5. When you walk across a rug, (positive, negative) charges can move from the rug to your shoes.

6. Use the phrases in the box to complete the diagram below.

negative charges move to it	**becomes negatively charged**
neutral before being rubbed by object	**negative charges move from it**
becomes positively charged	

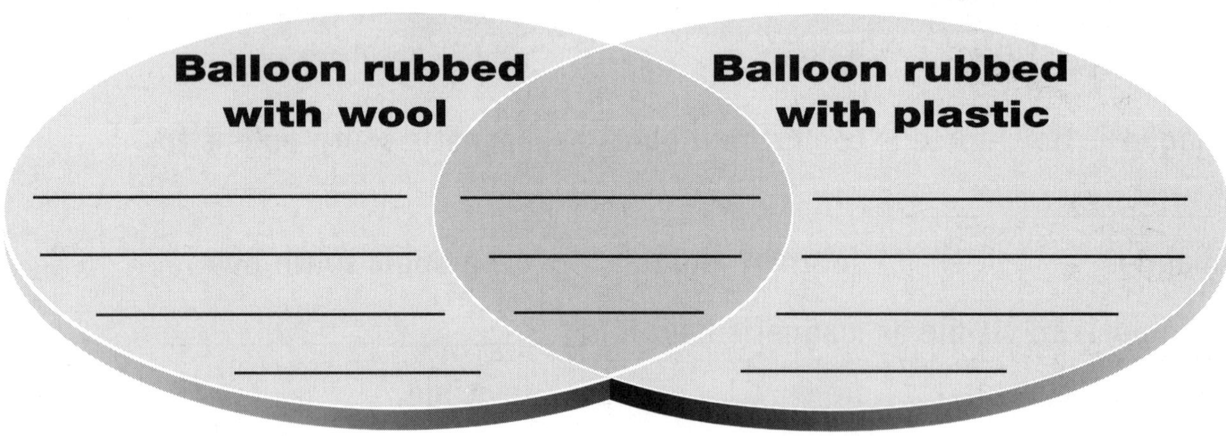

Process Skills

Communicating

List three ways you can practice lightning safety. Write your answers on a separate sheet of paper.

Name ______________________ Date ______________

Circle the word or words that best complete each sentence.

1. Electric charges must (remain still, flow) to be useful.

2. An electric current is a stream of (negative, positive) charges.

3. Charges move through a circuit that is (closed, open).

4. Electricity passes easily through (insulators, conductors).

5. Electricity powers a (faucet, flashlight).

6. Read the steps that describe the movement of electric charges in a closed circuit. The steps are not in the right order. Number them in the correct order.

____ Charges move through the light bulb.

____ Charges move through the wire leading back to the dry cell.

____ Charges leave the dry cell.

____ Charges move through the switch.

____ Charges move from the switch to the light bulb.

Process Skills

Predicting

What will happen to a buzzer connected to an open circuit? Explain your answer.

____

____

____

Investigation Review
How Do Electric Circuits Differ?

Name ______________________ Date ______________

Write the letter of the term that best matches the definition.

____	**1.** part of a light bulb that glows		**a.** parallel
____	**2.** bulb filled with mercury gas		**b.** fuse
____	**3.** bulb that produces two forms of energy		**c.** series
____	**4.** circuit connected in a single path		**d.** filament
____	**5.** circuit that has more than one path		**e.** circuit breaker
____	**6.** switch that opens a circuit by shutting off		**f.** fluorescent
____	**7.** device that opens a circuit by melting		**g.** incandescent

Each group of terms below contains one term that does not belong with the others. Cross out the term that doesn't belong.

8.	circuit breaker	series	fuse
9.	carbon	parallel	series
10.	filament	mercury	incandescent
11.	fluorescent	ultraviolet	tungsten
12.	lamps	fuse	flashlight

Process Skills
Inferring

Why might the electricity go off in the kitchen of a house if a number of kitchen appliances are running at the same time?

____

____

____

What Are Some Sources of Electric Current?

Name ______________________________ Date ____________________

Circle the word or words that best complete each sentence.

1. A device that uses a wire coil and a magnet to produce electricity is a (generator, battery).

2. In an electric cell, energy stored in (magnets, chemicals) changes to electrical energy.

3. The force that pushes electricity along wires is (charge, voltage).

A

4. A (transformer, generator) changes the voltage of a current.

5. Solar cells change (chemical energy, sunlight) to electrical energy.

B

6. Study the picture of an electricity experiment. Write O for each sentence that shows an observation. Write I for each sentence that shows an inference.

____ No current is flowing in pictures A and C.

____ The magnet is moving inside the cardboard tube in picture B.

____ A current is flowing through the wire in picture B.

____ The cause of the needle's movement in picture B is an electric current.

____ In picture C the magnet stops moving and so does the needle.

C

Process Skills

Making a Hypothesis

If you were going on a remote camping trip, which kind of items would you pack in your suitcase—items powered by electrical energy that comes from chemical energy or items that plug into a circuit? Why? Provide examples to illustrate your answer. Write your answer on a separate sheet of paper.

Name ______________________________ Date ____________________

Use the words in the box to complete each sentence.

electric	overloaded	electromagnet
batteries	fuses	

1. Electric cars do not pollute the air because they run on ________________.

2. Household appliances, such as refrigerators and vacuum cleaners, have ________________ motors.

3. When a coil of wire is wrapped around a nail and attached to a dry cell, the nail can become a(n) ________________.

4. A(n) ________________ circuit is always a safety hazard because wires can become very hot, which could cause a fire.

5. ________________ open circuits when wires get too hot.

6. Describe an electromagnet.

____

____

____

____

Process Skills

Communicating

What kinds of objects in your home or school contain electromagnets? Write your answer on a separate sheet of paper.